Resin Jewelry

Lori Wenger

LEISURE ARTS, INC. • Maumelle, Arkansas

Pink & white
Pink & gold
Ombre Color
Paper Confetti

Lori Wenger

Lori worked as a staff designer at Leisure Arts for more than seven years, contributing to books such as The Spirit of Christmas and Gooseberry Patch, among others. Since 2012, she has been a contributing photo stylist for numerous Leisure Arts publications. In her free time Lori enjoys relaxing with her family and friends and trying out fun, crafty projects with her kids. Check out other books by Lori including Tasseled Jewelry, Cool String Art, Boho Jewelry, and Aromatherapy Jewelry. Find her on Instagram at lori_wenger.

Contents

1

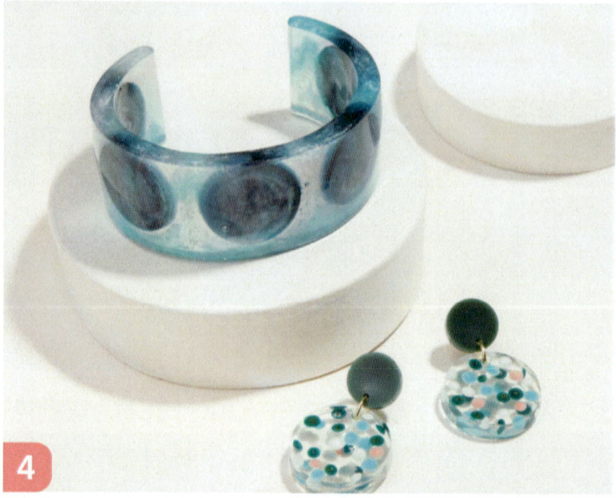

4

7

2

3

5

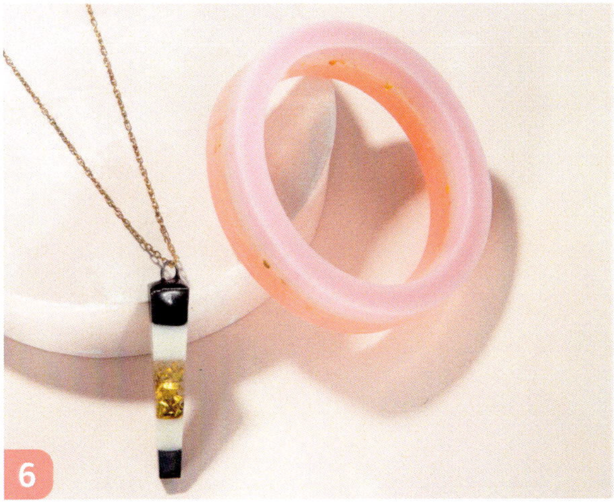
6

8

9

Introduction

WELCOME TO UV RESIN JEWELRY MAKING

Have you ever wanted to try to make your own resin jewelry but were intimidated by all of the mixing and measuring that seemed to go hand-in-hand with the craft? Well you have come to the right place. UV Resin is readily available and so easy to use. With no need to pre-mix with a special hardener and with the endless possibilities of things that can be added to your pieces, UV resin will open up an entirely new way for you to be able to express your inner artist. In this book we will be exploring a range of jewelry making techniques. We take you through the simple steps of basic molding, to more complex techniques required to achieve beautiful finished pieces of jewelry you will be proud to wear and to share as gifts with family and friends. The colors used to complete the projects in this book are shown as examples to illustrate the techniques we are exploring. The color choices and add-in options are yours, as the artist, to select.

Getting to Know Your Tools

This section is designed to familiarize you with the basic UV resin tools needed to create your jewelry.

UV Resin

UV resin is the key component used in making your jewelry pieces. Generally, you will be working with clear resin, but it is available in premixed colors from pearlized to opaque depending on what look you are trying to achieve. You can find it available to purchase online or at your local craft store. Play around with different colors and techniques that inspire your inner artist. UV resin cleans up easily with just soap and water.

Colorants and add-ins

There are a variety of options available to add color to your clear resin. From fine powders to alcohol inks and dyes. Read the labels and be sure that anything you are adding for coloring is designed to be used with UV resin specifically, as it is cured differently than epoxy resins. You can achieve beautiful color, shine, and sparkle in any piece by adding fine glitter, chunky glitter, confetti and many other options. Because UV resin is so versatile, you really can add just about anything you desire to create your personalized look and feel to any of your masterpieces. A little goes a long way when it comes to adding colors to your resin, too much may affect the drying time of your finished piece.

Silicone Molds and Silicone Mat

There are many different types of molds that are used in making UV resin jewelry. Some are sold as individual shapes while others come in sheets with many different shapes. If you are starting with a kit, they generally come with a variety of shapes and sizes. Keep in mind that the deeper your mold is and the larger your piece, curing times may take longer. You want to be sure you are working over a silicone mat for easy clean-up of your workstation. Any spills or drips can be cured and used as add-in pieces for your projects or simply removed and discarded once they have dried.

UV Lamps

Your UV lamp is an important tool when making jewelry using UV resin. Read the instructions on your UV resin to see if there is a specific wattage of lamp that needs to be used to cure your product and the recommended time to expose your piece to the light for complete curing. Most UV resins require a general UV lamp that will come with the light source that you need. UV resin can also be cured using the UV rays of the sunlight but it takes considerably longer. Using a toothpick, poke an edge of your piece in an inconspicuous spot to see if it has cured. It should be hard and not tacky at all. If you find that a piece hasn't completely cured after you have had it under the lamp, you can finish it off in sunlight or with a UV flashlight. When you are curing your piece, whether under a lamp or in the sunlight, always be sure it is done on a level surface.

Pre-formed Jewelry Elements

Many of the projects we will be creating in this book are done by pouring resin directly into a pre-formed jewelry element, also known as open or closed bezel pieces. The open bezel pieces allow you to admire your work from both sides. To create a surface to pour the resin into when using an open bezel piece, simply place a piece of clear tape to the back side, being sure to press around the edges so the resin doesn't leak from the sides. The tape can easily be removed once your piece is completely cured. The closed bezel pieces have a closed back that gives you a surface to pour into. These are the best types to use when you are including pictures into your jewelry piece.

Supplies List

As with any project you are undertaking it is important to have all the supplies you will need before you get started. This is especially true when working with a wet medium such as UV resin. We have listed the general supplies you need to re-create the projects in this book. You are the artist here and your creations do not have to be limited to what we have used. Check out all the options available at your local craft store or online.

GENERAL SUPPLIES

- Clear UV Resin
- UV Lamp
- Molds
- Plastic Gloves
- Silicone Mixing Cups
- Stirring Sticks
- Spoons
- Tweezers
- Silicone Mat
- Wand Lighter *(BBQ lighter or candle lighter)*
- UV Flashlight *(optional)*
- Clear Packing Tape
- Toothpick
- Small Paintbrush *(tip of handle used for creating dots)*

COLORANTS AND ADD-IN SUPPLIES

- Fine and Chunky Glitter
- Alcohol Ink
- Pearlizing Powder
- Color Powders
- Cardstock in White and in a variety of colors
- Acrylic Paint
- Confetti

JEWELRY MAKING MATERIALS

- Open Bezel Pendant Charms
- Closed Back Bezel Bracelet
- Jump Rings
- Necklace Chains
- Earring Hooks
- Flat Surface Earring Studs
- Decorative Earring Posts *(with loop for jump ring)*
- Clasps *(for necklace chains if not included with chain)*
- Jewelry Pliers
- Jewelry Snips
- Paper Strip *(for measuring ring size)*
- Ruler
- Marker
- Fine Grit Sandpaper

Ring Sizing Information

In this book, we make a variety of different rings. You can find ring molds for different styles that include every size, so it is important to know your ring size. Below we have included a few options for measuring ring sizes and a sizing chart for your reference.

Option 1:

Wrap a thin strip of paper around your finger where you want your ring to rest. Mark paper where it first overlaps itself. Measure the paper in millimeters and divide the number of millimeters measured by 3.14. Example: You measured 50 mm ÷ 3.14 = 15.92 mm which translates to ring size 5.5. Check chart for appropriate ring size based on the measured millimeters. If your knuckle is larger than the area you measured, you may want to go up a half ring size to be sure your ring can get past your knuckle.

Option 2:

You can use a ring that currently fits you and measure for the right size ring mold to use.

Option 3:

If you are going to be making a number of rings you may want to invest in your own ring-measurement tool. There are many inexpensive options available at your local craft store or online.

Common ring sizes for women are 6 (16.5 mm), 6.5 (16.9 mm), and 7 (17.3 mm). For men the most common sizes are 10 (19.8 mm), 10.5 (20.2 mm), and 11 (20.6 mm).

Millimeters	Ring Size	Millimeters	Ring Size
14 mm	3	18.6 mm	8.5
14.4 mm	3.5	19 mm	9
14.8 mm	4	19.4 mm	9.5
15.2 mm	4.5	19.8 mm	10
15.6 mm	5	20.2 mm	10.5
16 mm	5.5	20.6 mm	11
16.45 mm	6	21 mm	11.5
16.9 mm	6.5	21.4 mm	12
17.3 mm	7	21.8 mm	12.5
17.7 mm	7.5	22.2 mm	13
18.2 mm	8	22.6 mm	13.5

General Resin Molding Instructions

In this section we will be walking you step-by-step through working with UV Resin to successfully create Resin Jewelry pieces. If you are a first time UV resin jewelry maker, I recommend starting on pieces that are poured into molds before you jump into pouring into bezel pendant charms. Getting comfortable working with UV resin will make the more complex pieces much less intimidating. So, let's get started.

Step 1: Gather your supplies and lay out your silicone mat. Be sure you wear gloves to protect your hands while working ***(photos A, B and C)***.

Step 2: Add resin to silicone mixing cup ***(photo D)***.

Step 3: Add color. There are a few options available at this step. Alcohol ink, pearlizing and color powders. Whichever method you choose, be sure to stir your mixture well using your stir stick. This step is also when you can add glitter, confetti, etc. if you are wanting them to fall randomly in your piece ***(photos E and F)***.

A

B

C

D

E

F

PRO-TIP:

When adding color, a little goes a long way.
Too much will affect the time it takes for your piece to cure.

Step 4: Pour resin mixture into mold being sure to fill to top as it does not expand. If you are going to add large pieces such as confetti or chunky glitter, fill almost to top. Once you have added your "bling", fill remaining space in mold and re-adjust the placement of your pieces with tweezers if they have shifted ***(photo G)***.

Step 5: Add in the fun! Using tweezers, add confetti, chunky glitter or whatever else you want to include in your masterpiece. See step 5 for making sure to bring resin to top of mold ***(photo H)***.

Step 6: Quickly skim the top of the resin with a flame from a lighter to remove any bubbles from the surface ***(photo I)***.

Step 7: Set under UV light for 2 to 4 minutes or as directed on your resin instructions ***(photo J)***. Flip the mold to make sure the bottom has a solid cure. If your piece is tacky to the touch, it isn't fully cured. Set it in sunlight for 20 minutes to an hour to allow it to fully cure (harden).

G

H

I

PRO-TIP:

Use a toothpick to gently touch your piece in an inconspicuous spot to feel for tackiness. You don't want to leave a fingerprint.

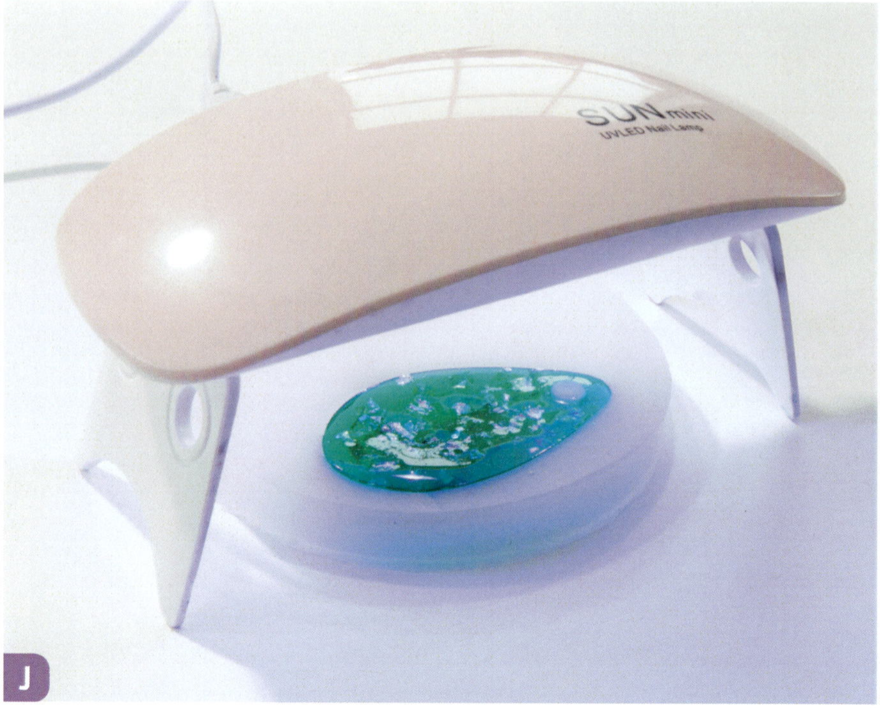

J

Step 8: Once completely cured, remove resin from mold ***(photo K)***.

Step 9: Add jewelry elements ***(photo L)***.

Step 10: Admire your beautiful creation ***(photo M)***.

Note: *Your finished piece may end up with a sharp edge on it where it rested against the mold. It may even have a slight dip on the top surface. You can remedy this by either adding an additional thin resin layer to fill the dip, or you can simply sand the edges with a fine grit sandpaper to eliminate the sharp edge.*

K

L

M

1

Basic Molding Projects
WITH NO ADD-INS

Most of the projects we have included in this book use more complex techniques than just basic molding. In this section we wanted to showcase the beauty that can be obtained using even the simplest, most basic mix and pour technique.

SUPPLIES

- Clear UV Resin
- Colorant or Pre-colored Resin
- UV Lamp
- Silicone Molds
- Plastic Gloves
- Silicone Mixing Cups
- Silicone Mat
- Stirring Sticks
- Toothpick
- Paper Strip *(for measuring ring size)*
- Ruler
- Marker
- Fine Grit Sandpaper

Basic Molding

Refer to Ring Sizing Information on page 11 if you have selected ring molds to complete the projects in this section.

Step 1: Decide which mold shape you are going to use. We have used two different styled ring molds. Gather your supplies and lay out your silicone mat. Be sure you wear gloves to protect your hands while working.

Step 2: Add resin to silicone mixing cup. If you are using a pre-colored resin, proceed to Step 4.

Step 3: Add color. There are a few options available at this step. Alcohol ink, pearlizing, and color powders. Whichever method you choose, be sure to stir your mixture well using your stir stick.

Step 4: Pour resin mixture into mold being sure to fill to top as it does not expand.

Step 5: Quickly skim the top of the resin with a flame from a lighter to remove any bubbles from the surface.

Step 6: Set under UV light for 2 to 4 minutes or as directed on your resin instructions. Flip the mold to make sure the bottom has a solid cure. Before you remove your piece from the mold, touch an inconspicuous place with a toothpick to be sure it has completely cured. If piece is still tacky, place in sunlight until hardened. Once completely hardened remove from mold.

Step 7: If your piece has a slight dip on top, fill this area with a small layer of resin and allow to harden in sunlight. Sand any sharp edges if needed with fine grit sand paper.

Step 8: Add any jewelry elements needed to complete your piece.

Note: Your finished piece may end up with a sharp edge on it where it rested against the mold. It may even have a slight dip on the top surface. You can remedy this by either adding an additional thin resin layer to fill the dip, or you can simply sand the edges with a fine grit sandpaper to eliminate the sharp edge.

2

Basic Molding Projects
WITH ADD-INS

This section is designed to show off the beautiful pieces that even the simplest molding techniques can achieve. Some of our add-in glitter is mixed in a small amount with clear UV resin and poured, while other pieces have had the glitter placed in specific places. Both looks come out stunning.

SUPPLIES

- Clear UV Resin
- Colorant or Pre-colored Resin
- UV Lamp
- Silicone Molds
- Plastic Gloves
- Silicone Mixing Cups
- Silicone Mat
- Tweezers
- Toothpick
- Fine Grit Sandpaper
- Chunky Gold Glitter
- Medium Gold Glitter
- Flat Earring Studs *(if you are making studded earrings)*
- Pendant Holder Style Necklace Charm
- Necklace Chain *(if it doesn't come with necklace charm)*
- Jump Rings
- Jewelry Pliers
- Jewelry Snips

Gold Glitter and Clear Ring and Earrings

Step 1: Decide which mold shape you are going to use. We used open circle hoop style molds for the earrings and raised ring mold. Gather your supplies and lay out your silicone mat. Be sure you wear gloves to protect your hands while working.

Step 2: Pour clear resin into your earring and ring molds filling only 3/4 of the way to the top.

Step 3: With tweezers, place the chunky gold glitter pieces into molds at desired positions and as many as you want. Fill remaining space of molds with more clear resin and re-adjust confetti pieces if they have shifted.

Step 4: Quickly skim the top of the resin with a flame from a lighter to remove any bubbles from the surface.

Step 5: Set your pieces under the UV light for 2 to 4 minutes or as directed on your resin instructions. Flip the molds to make sure the bottom has a solid cure. Before you remove your pieces from the molds, touch an inconspicuous place with a toothpick to be sure they have completely cured. If pieces are still tacky, place in sunlight until hardened. Once completely hardened remove from molds.

A

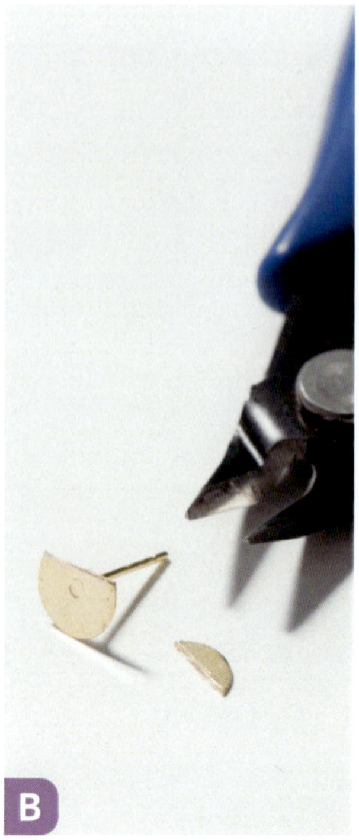
B

Step 6: If your pieces have a slight dip on top, fill this area with a small layer of resin and allow to harden in sunlight. Sand any sharp edges if needed with fine grit sand paper.

Step 7: Glue the open end of your hoop onto earring studs. These can be glued onto your piece using a drop of clear resin ***(photo A)***.

If you need to, you can snip the edges of the earring studs to fit end of hoops ***(photo B)***.

Step 8: Place earring under UV lamp for 1–2 minutes to cure "glue drop".

Gold Glitter and Clear Pendant

Step 1: Decide which mold shape you are going to use. We used a large teardrop shaped mold. Gather your supplies and lay out your silicone mat. Be sure you wear gloves to protect your hands while working.

Step 2: In a silicone mixing cup, stir in a small amount of medium gold glitter into clear resin and mix well.

Step 3: Fill mold to top with mixture.

Step 4: Quickly skim the top of the resin with a flame from a lighter to remove any bubbles from the surface.

Step 5: Set your piece under the UV light for 2 to 4 minutes or as directed on your resin instructions. Flip the mold to make sure the bottom has a solid cure. Before you remove your piece from the mold, touch an inconspicuous place with a toothpick to be sure it has completely cured. If piece is still tacky, place in sunlight until hardened. Once completely hardened remove from mold.

Step 6: If your piece has a slight dip on top, fill this area with a small layer of resin and allow to harden in sunlight. Sand any sharp edges if needed with fine grit sand paper.

Step 7: Using jewelry pliers, attach jump ring to top of pendant and to jewelry charm. If you have chosen a different style to make, attach your jewelry elements accordingly.

Milky Pink Oval Earrings

Step 1: Decide which mold shape you are going to use. We used flat baseball diamond shaped molds with hole stems for earring studs and open oval molds with hole stems for earrings. Be sure the flat circles are large enough be glued onto earring studs without covering the hole. If you need to, you can snip the edges of the earring studs to fit ***(photo B)***. Gently sand cut edge so it is not rough against your ear. Gather your supplies and lay out your silicone mat. Be sure you wear gloves to protect your hands while working.

Step 2: Pour clear resin into your flat circle molds filling only ¾ of the way to the top.

Step 3: With tweezers, place the chunky gold glitter pieces into molds at desired positions and as many as you want. Fill remaining space of molds with more clear resin and re-adjust confetti pieces if they have shifted.

Step 4: Quickly skim the top of the resin with a flame from a lighter to remove any bubbles from the surface.

Step 5: Set your pieces under the UV light for 2 to 4 minutes or as directed on your resin instructions. Flip the molds to make sure the bottom has a solid cure. Before you remove your pieces from the molds, touch an inconspicuous place with a toothpick to be sure they have completely cured. If pieces are still tacky, place in sunlight until hardened. Once completely hardened remove from molds.

Step 6: If your pieces have a slight dip on top, fill this area with a small layer of resin and allow to harden in sunlight. Sand any sharp edges if needed with fine grit sand paper.

Step 7: Glue the small flat resin circles onto earring studs being careful not to cover the hole. These can be glued onto your piece using a drop of clear resin ***(photo A)***.

Step 8: Place earring studs under UV lamp for 1–2 minutes to cure "glue drop". Set aside.

Step 9: Pour colored resin into your oval molds.

Step 10: Quickly skim the top of the resin with a flame from a lighter to remove any bubbles from the surface.

Step 11: Set your pieces under the UV light for 2 to 4 minutes or as directed on your resin instructions. Flip the molds to make sure the bottom has a solid cure. Before you remove your pieces from the molds, touch an inconspicuous place with a toothpick to be sure they have completely cured. If pieces are still tacky, place in sunlight until hardened. Once completely hardened remove from molds.

Step 12: If your pieces have a slight dip on top, fill this area with a small layer of resin and allow to harden in sunlight. Sand any sharp edges if needed with fine grit sand paper.

Step 13: Using jewelry pliers, attach jump rings to connect the studs to oval earrings. If you have chosen a different style to make, attach your jewelry elements accordingly.

3

Dot Painting
TECHNIQUE

The technique of dot painting is as simple as it sounds. Using two different colors of resin or even two different shades of a similar color, you can give your jewelry piece added depth without any add-ins. We have done earrings in green with white dots to showcase the technique. This technique can be applied in any shape or color you desire.

SUPPLIES

- Clear UV Resin
- Colorant or Pre-colored Resin
- UV Lamp
- Silicone Molds
- Plastic Gloves
- Silicone Mixing Cups
- Silicone Mat
- Stirring Sticks
- Toothpick
- Small Paintbrush *(handle used for creating dots)*
- Fine Grit Sandpaper
- Flat Earring Studs *(if you are making studded earrings)*
- Jewelry Elements needed to complete your piece

Green Earrings with White Polka Dots

Step 1: Decide which mold shape you are going to use. We have used horseshoe shaped molds. Gather your supplies and lay out your silicone mat. Be sure you wear gloves to protect your hands while working.

Step 2: Mix the resin colors you have selected to use.

Step 3: Before you pour the main color of resin into your desired mold shape, dip the handle end of your paintbrush into secondary resin color and place dots where you want them in your mold ***(photo A)***.

Step 4: Place mold with only the dots under the UV lamp for 1 minute.

Step 5: Pour your main color resin into mold to fill.

Step 6: Quickly skim the top of the resin with a flame from a lighter to remove any bubbles from the surface.

Step 7: Cure your piece under the UV lamp for the directed amount of time on your resin instructions.

Step 8: Before you remove your piece from the mold, touch an inconspicuous place with a toothpick to be sure it has completely cured. If piece is still tacky, place in sunlight until hardened. Once completely hardened remove from mold.

Step 9: If your piece has a slight dip on top, fill this area with a small layer of resin and allow to harden in sunlight. Sand any sharp edges if needed with fine grit sand paper.

Step 10: Add any jewelry elements needed to complete your piece.

Note: We used flat earring studs for our piece. These can be glued onto your piece using a drop of clear resin ***(photo B)***. Cure your pieces under UV lamp after you have glued studs into place.

A

B

4

Resin Inside Resin
TECHNIQUE

Similar to the painting with dots technique, the resin inside resin technique utilizes different colored resin shapes as add-ins. This technique allows you, as the artist, to utilize any shape you desire to include in your jewelry. Rather than relying solely on pre-shaped pieces, your imagination can be expressed in any shape or color. In this section, we have created a few different pieces showing this technique used in molding resin in silicone as well as it being utilized in open and closed bezel pieces. The color choices are yours to decide as well as how you want to apply this technique. The possibilities are endless so have fun with it.

SUPPLIES

- Clear UV Resin
- Colorant or Pre-colored Resin
- Translucent UV Resin in 2 colors *(for open sided bracelet)*
- UV Lamp
- Silicone Molds
- Silicone Mixing Cups
- Silicone Mat
- Stirring Sticks
- Toothpick
- Clear Packing Tape
- Fine Grit Sandpaper
- Small Paintbrush *(handle used for creating dots)*
- Tweezers
- Bezel Pendants
- Bezel Bracelet Form
- Jump Rings
- Jewelry Pliers
- Jewelry Snips
- Jewelry Elements needed to complete your pieces

The jewelry elements we used to complete our pieces are as follows:

Circle Polka Dot Earrings—we used flat earring studs and jump rings.

Pink, Green and White Set—we used an open bezel pendant for necklace *(along with chain and jump ring)*; open bezel pendants for earrings *(along with earring hooks and jump rings)* and a closed bezel bracelet form.

Teal Bracelet with Circles Inside

Step 1: Decide which molds you are going to use. We used circle molds as well as an open sided bracelet mold. Gather your supplies and lay out your silicone mat. Be sure you wear gloves to protect your hands while working.

Step 2: Mix the resin color you have selected to use for your circles.

Step 3: Pour resin into circle molds.

Step 4: Quickly skim the top of the resin with a flame from a lighter to remove any bubbles from the surface.

Step 5: Set your pieces under the UV light for 2 to 4 minutes or as directed on your resin instructions. Flip the molds to make sure the bottom has a solid cure. Before you remove your pieces from the mold, touch an inconspicuous place with a toothpick to be sure they have completely cured. If pieces are still tacky, place in sunlight until hardened. Once completely hardened remove from molds.

Step 6: If your pieces have a slight dip on top, fill this area with a small layer of resin and allow to harden in sunlight.

Step 7: Place your circles into the bracelet mold ***(photo A and B)***.

Step 8: Pour two different colors of translucent resins inside bracelet mold, layering them as you pour.

Step 9: Quickly skim the top of the resin with a flame from a lighter to remove any bubbles from the surface.

Step 10: Set your piece under the UV light for 2 to 4 minutes or as directed on your resin instructions. Flip the mold to make sure the bottom has a solid cure. Before you remove your piece from the mold, touch an inconspicuous place with a toothpick to be sure it has completely cured. If piece is still tacky, place in sunlight until hardened. Once completely hardened remove from mold. Because this mold is deep, it may take a bit longer to cure.

Step 11: If your piece has a slight dip on top, fill this area with a small layer of resin and allow to harden in sunlight. Sand any sharp edges if needed with fine grit sand paper.

A

B

Circle Polka Dot Earrings

Step 1: Decide which molds you are going to use. We used two different sized circle molds with hole stems. Be sure the smaller size you are going to use to glue to the earring studs are large enough to be glued into place without covering the hole. If you need to, you can snip the edges of the earring studs to fit ***(photo C)***. Gently sand cut edge so it is not rough against your ear. Gather your supplies and lay out your silicone mat. Be sure you wear gloves to protect your hands while working.

Step 2: Mix the resin color you have selected to use for your earring stud circles.

Step 3: Pour resin into circle molds.

Step 4: Quickly skim the top of the resin with a flame from a lighter to remove any bubbles from the surface.

Step 5: Set your piece under the UV light for 2 to 4 minutes or as directed on your resin instructions. Flip the mold to make sure the bottom has a solid cure. Before you remove your piece from the mold, touch an inconspicuous place with a toothpick to be sure it has completely cured. If piece is still tacky, place in sunlight until hardened. Once completely hardened remove from mold.

Step 6: Set aside.

Step 7: Using the end of your paintbrush and the flat side of any silicone mold, make tiny polka dots with colored resin. Place under UV lamp and cure completely. Once cured, scrape off of mold to use as add-ins for earring circles and set aside ***(photo D)***.

Step 8: Pour clear resin into the larger hole stemmed circle molds filling only ¾ of the way to the top.

C

D

Step 9: With tweezers, place the small dots you made with paintbrush tip into circle molds. Fill remaining space of molds with more clear resin ***(photo E)***.

Step 10: Quickly skim the top of the resin with a flame from a lighter to remove any bubbles from the surface.

Step 11: Set your piece under the UV light for 2 to 4 minutes or as directed on your resin instructions. Flip the mold to make sure the bottom has a solid cure. Before you remove your piece from the mold, touch an inconspicuous place with a toothpick to be sure it has completely cured. If piece is still tacky, place in sunlight until hardened. Once completely hardened remove from mold.

Step 12: If your pieces have a slight dip on top, fill this area with a small layer of resin and allow to harden in sunlight. Sand any sharp edges if needed with fine grit sand paper.

Step 13: Glue the small flat resin circles onto earring studs being careful not to cover the hole. These can be glued onto your piece using a drop of clear resin ***(photo F)***.

Step 14: Place earring studs under UV lamp for 1–2 minutes to cure "glue drop".

Step 15: Using jewelry pliers, attach jump rings to connect the studs to your polka dot circles. If you have chosen a different style to make, attach your jewelry elements accordingly.

Pink, Green, and White Jewelry Set

The Earrings

Step 1: Decide which bezel shape you are going to use. We used teardrop shaped open bezel pendants. Gather your supplies and lay out your silicone mat. Be sure you wear gloves to protect your hands while working.

Step 2: Using the end of your paintbrush and the flat side of any silicone mold, make the desired size polka dots with different colored resin than what you will be using for background color. Place under UV lamp and cure completely. Once cured, scrape off of mold. Set aside ***(photo G)***.

Step 3: Mix the resin color you have chosen as your background color for your earrings.

Step 4: Apply a piece of clear packing tape to the back of each of the open bezel pendants. Be sure the tape is pressed well to the edges of your pendant so that no resin will leak through.

Step 5: Add a thin layer of colored resin to the inside of each of the bezel pendants being sure the resin goes all the way to the edge ***(photo H)***.

Step 6: Quickly skim the top of the resin with a flame from a lighter to remove any bubbles from the surface.

Step 7: Set your piece under the UV light for 2 to 4 minutes or as directed on your resin instructions. Touch an inconspicuous place with a toothpick to be sure it has completely cured. If piece is still tacky, place in sunlight until hardened. Once completely hardened remove tape from pendants.

G

H

Step 8: Using clear resin as glue, apply a drop to flat side of dots and place dots on top of thin layered pendants. Cure under UV lamp again.

Step 9: Pour clear resin over the entire inside of the pendant to fill.

Step 10: Quickly skim the top of the resin with a flame from a lighter to remove any bubbles from the surface.

Step 11: Set your piece under the UV light for 2 to 4 minutes or as directed on your resin instructions. Touch an inconspicuous place on each pendant with a toothpick to be sure they have completely cured. If pieces are still tacky, place in sunlight until hardened.

Step 12: If your piece has a slight dip on top, fill this area with a small layer of resin and allow to harden in sunlight.

Step 13: Connect the pendants to ring at base of earring hooks. If you have chosen a different style to make, attach your jewelry elements accordingly.

The Necklace

Steps 1–12: Follow steps 1–12 of Earring instructions above being sure to make 2 smaller dots and 1 larger dot to duplicate the look of our piece. You are the artist and can use this technique to use whatever size dots or shapes you want ***(photo I and J)***.

Step 13: Using jewelry pliers, attach a jump ring to secure pendant to necklace chain.

The Bracelet

Step 1: Decide which bezel shape you are going to use. We used a closed back, watch style bezel bracelet. Gather your supplies and lay out your silicone mat. Be sure you wear gloves to protect your hands while working.

Step 2: Using the end of your paintbrush and the flat side of any silicone mold, make one large dot in your color choice, and the number of smaller dots needed to fill the space of bezel in contrasting

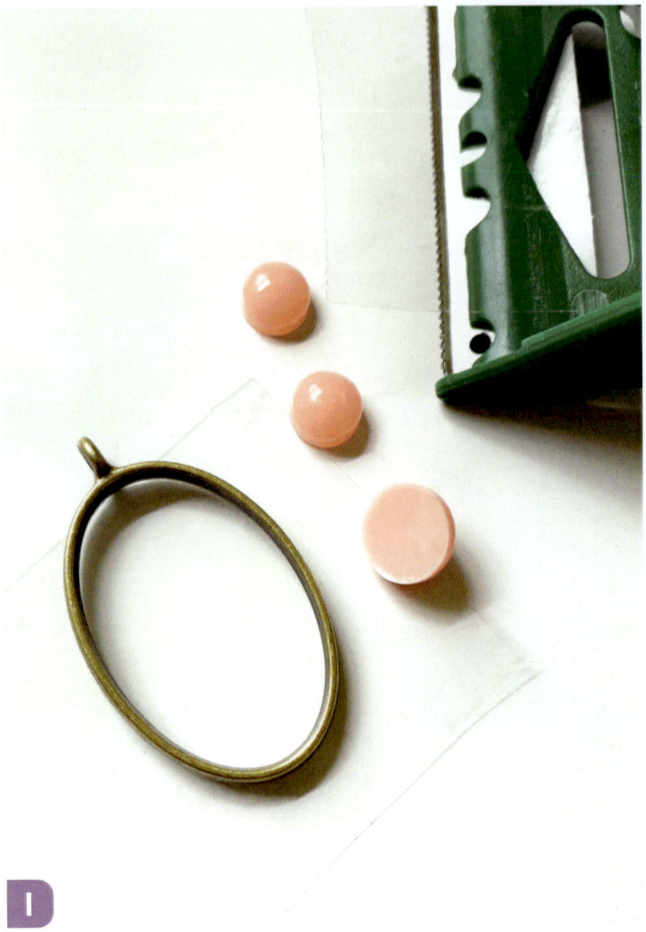

I

J

color (we added 11). Place under UV lamp and cure completely. Once cured, scrape off of mold. Set aside ***(photo K)***.

Step 3: Add a thin layer of colored or clear resin to the inside of the bezel bracelet being sure the resin goes all the way to the edge.

Step 4: Set your piece under the UV light for 2 to 4 minutes or as directed on your resin instructions.

Step 5: Touch an inconspicuous place on bracelet with a toothpick to be sure it has completely cured. If piece is still tacky, place in sunlight until hardened.

Step 6: Arrange resin dots inside bracelet to be sure they fit properly before gluing into place ***(photo L)***.

Step 7: Using clear resin as glue, place a drop of resin to flat side of dots and arrange in place inside bracelet. Cure under UV lamp again.

Step 8: Pour clear resin over the entire inside of the dot filled bracelet cup to fill.

Step 9: Quickly skim the top of the resin with a flame from a lighter to remove any bubbles from the surface.

Step 10: Set your piece under the UV light for 2 to 4 minutes or as directed on your resin instructions. Touch an inconspicuous place on bracelet with a toothpick to be sure it has completely cured. If piece is still tacky, place in sunlight until hardened.

Step 11: If your piece has a slight dip on top, fill this area with a small layer of resin and allow to harden in sunlight.

K

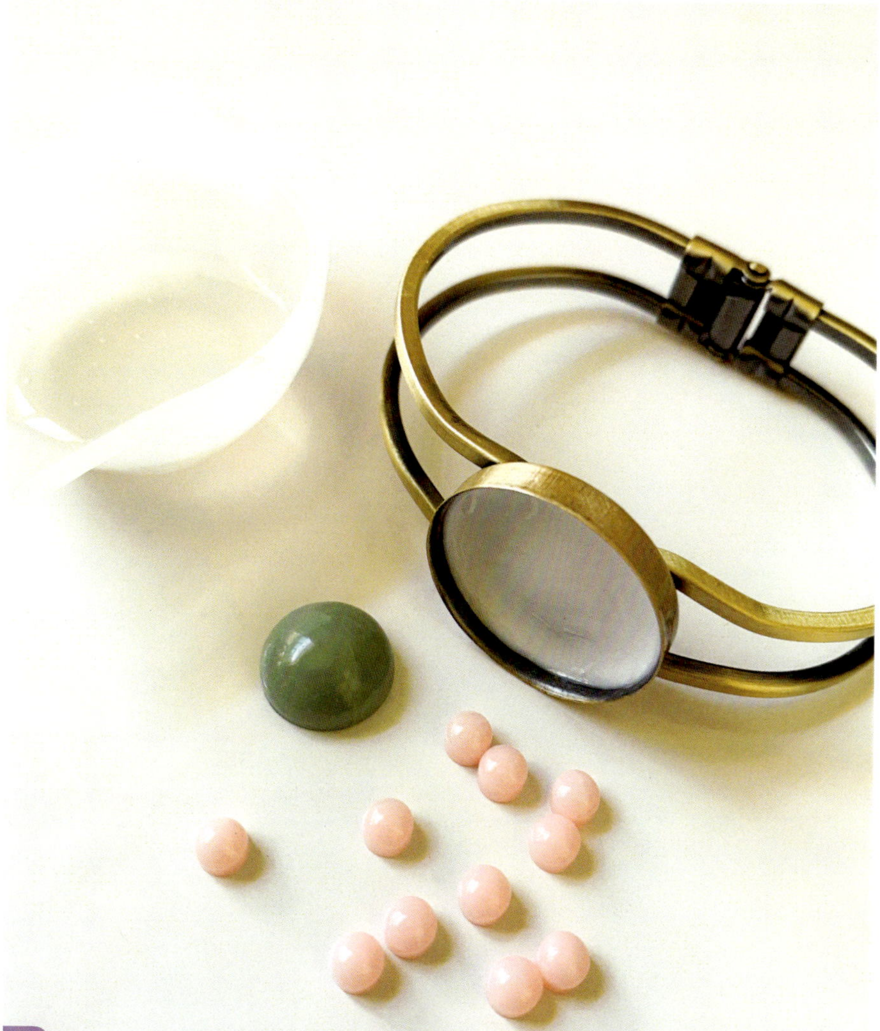

L

5

Paper Confetti
TECHNIQUE

The paper confetti technique opens up a wonderful way to add very precise color components to any of your resin projects. It can be applied in both clear and colored resin, creating endless possibilities of ways to express your creative self.

SUPPLIES

- Clear UV Resin
- 2 colors of translucent white resin *(if you are choosing to duplicate our rectangle pendant)*
- UV Lamp
- Silicone Molds
- Plastic Gloves
- Silicone Mixing Cups
- Silicone Mat
- Tweezers
- Toothpick
- Fine Grit Sandpaper
- Variety of Cardstock colors *(cut into confetti; your choice in size and shape)*
- White Cardstock *(cut into confetti; small amount needed for 5 square pendant)*
- Flat Earring Studs *(if you are making studded earrings)*
- Rectangle Closed Bezel Pendant
- Necklace Chain
- Jump Rings
- Jewelry Pliers
- Jewelry Snips

Colorful Confetti Bracelet and Ring

Step 1: Decide which mold shape you are going to use. We used a rounded bracelet mold and a flat sided ring mold. Gather your supplies and lay out your silicone mat. Be sure you wear gloves to protect your hands while working.

Step 2: Pour clear resin into your bracelet and ring molds filling only 3/4 of the way to the top.

Step 3: With tweezers, place the colorful confetti pieces into molds at desired positions and as many as you want. Fill remaining space of molds with more clear resin and re-adjust confetti pieces if they have shifted ***(photo A)***.

Step 4: Quickly skim the top of the resin with a flame from a lighter to remove any bubbles from the surface.

Step 5: Set your pieces under the UV light for 2 to 4 minutes or as directed on your resin instructions. Flip the molds to make sure the bottom has a solid cure. Before you remove your pieces from the molds, touch an inconspicuous place with a toothpick to be sure they have completely cured. If pieces are still tacky, place in sunlight until hardened. Once completely hardened remove from molds.

Step 6: If your pieces have a slight dip on top, fill this area with a small layer of resin and allow to harden in sunlight. Sand any sharp edges if needed with fine grit sand paper.

Colorful Confetti Earrings

Step 1: Decide which mold shape you are going to use. We used flat circle molds with hole stems for earring studs and open oval molds with hole stems for earrings. Be sure the flat circles are large enough be glued onto earring studs without covering the hole. If you need to, you can snip the edges of the earring studs to fit ***(photo B)***. Gently sand cut edge so it is not rough against your ear. Gather your supplies and lay out your silicone mat. Be sure you wear gloves to protect your hands while working.

A

Step 2: Pour clear resin into your flat circle and open oval molds filling only 3/4 of the way to the top.

Step 3: With tweezers, place the colorful confetti pieces into molds at desired positions and as many as you want. Fill remaining space of molds with more clear resin and re-adjust confetti pieces if they have shifted.

Step 4: Quickly skim the top of the resin with a flame from a lighter to remove any bubbles from the surface.

Step 5: Set your pieces under the UV light for 2 to 4 minutes or as directed on your resin instructions. Flip the molds to make sure the bottom has a solid cure. Before you remove your pieces from the molds, touch an inconspicuous place with a toothpick to be sure they have completely cured. If pieces are still tacky, place in sunlight until hardened. Once completely hardened remove from molds.

Step 6: If your pieces have a slight dip on top, fill this area with a small layer of resin and allow to harden in sunlight. Sand any sharp edges if needed with fine grit sand paper.

Step 7: Glue the small flat resin circles onto earring studs being careful not to cover the hole. These can be glued onto your piece using a drop of clear resin ***(Photo C)***.

Step 8: Place earring studs under UV lamp for 1–2 minutes to cure "glue drop".

Step 9: Using jewelry pliers, attach jump rings to connect the studs to your polka dot circles. If you have chosen a different style to make, attach your jewelry elements accordingly.

5 White Squares Pendant

Step 1: Decide which bezel and mold shape you are going to use. We used a closed back, rectangle bezel pendant and square molds to fit inside of rectangle pendant. Gather your supplies and lay out your silicone mat. Be sure you wear gloves to protect your hands while working.

Step 2: Pour two different colors of translucent resins inside square molds, layering them as you pour and filling only 3/4 of the way to the top.

Step 3: With tweezers, place the white confetti pieces into molds at desired positions and as many as you want. Fill remaining space of molds following the same procedure used in Step 3 and re-adjust confetti pieces if they have shifted.

Step 4: Quickly skim the top of the resin with a flame from a lighter to remove any bubbles from the surface.

Step 5: Set your piece under the UV light for 2 to 4 minutes or as directed on your resin instructions. Flip the mold to make sure the bottom has a solid cure. Before you remove your piece from the mold, touch an inconspicuous place with a toothpick to be sure it has completely cured. If piece is still tacky, place in sunlight until hardened. Once completely hardened remove from mold.

Step 6: If your piece has a slight dip on top, fill this area with a small layer of resin and allow to harden in sunlight. Set Aside.

Step 7: Add a thin layer of colored or clear resin to the inside of the bezel pendant being sure the resin goes all the way to the edge.

Step 8: Cure your pendant under the UV lamp for the directed amount of time on your resin instructions.

Step 9: Touch an inconspicuous place on pendant with a toothpick to be sure it has completely cured. If piece is still tacky, place in sunlight until hardened.

Step 10: Arrange squares inside pendant to be sure they fit properly before gluing into place.

Step 11: Using clear resin as glue, place a drop of resin to flat side of squares and arrange in place inside pendant. Cure under UV lamp again.

Step 12: Using jewelry pliers, attach jump ring to secure pendant to necklace chain.

6

Layered Resin
TECHNIQUE

As you can see in the design pieces we have created, the layered resin technique allows you the artist to combine colors and add-in combinations in a very neat and orderly fashion. This technique allows you to build colors inside of a single piece without bleeding and blending into themselves. As with all of the techniques in this book, it can be applied to any shape and colors you choose.

SUPPLIES

- Clear UV Resin
- Colorant or Pre-colored Resin
- Chunky Gold Glitter
- UV Lamp
- Silicone Molds
- Plastic Gloves
- Silicone Mixing Cups
- Silicone Mat
- Tweezers
- Toothpick
- Fine Grit Sandpaper
- Necklace Chain
- Jump Ring
- Jewelry Pliers

Triple Tone Pink Bracelet

Step 1: Decide which mold shape you are going to use. We used a flat sided bracelet mold. Gather your supplies and lay out your silicone mat. Be sure you wear gloves to protect your hands while working.

Step 2: Mix the resin colors you have selected to use for your bracelet.

Step 3: Pour first color resin into bracelet mold filling ⅓ of the way up.

Step 4: Quickly skim the top of the resin with a flame from a lighter to remove any bubbles from the surface.

Step 5: Cure your bracelet under the UV lamp for 1 minute. You do not want the resin to be fully cured because it will begin to pull away from the mold. You just want the surface to be a little firm so colors don't mix.

Step 6: Pour second color resin into bracelet mold filling the next ⅓ of the way up.

Step 7: Quickly skim the top of the resin with a flame from a lighter to remove any bubbles from the surface.

Step 8: Cure your bracelet under the UV lamp for 1 minute.

Step 9: Fill remaining space of bracelet mold with third color.

Step 10: Quickly skim the top of the resin with a flame from a lighter to remove any bubbles from the surface.

Step 11: Set your piece under the UV light for 2 to 4 minutes or as directed on your resin instructions. Flip the mold to make sure the bottom has a solid cure. Before you remove your piece from the mold, touch an inconspicuous place with a toothpick to be sure it has completely cured. If piece is still tacky, place in sunlight until hardened. Once completely hardened remove from mold. Deeper molds may take longer to cure.

Step 12: If your piece has a slight dip on top, fill this area with a small layer of resin and allow to harden in sunlight. Sand any sharp edges if needed with fine grit sand paper.

Black, White, and Gold Pendant

Step 1: Decide which mold shape you are going to use. We used a spire mold. Gather your supplies and lay out your silicone mat. Be sure you wear gloves to protect your hands while working.

Step 2: Mix the resin colors you have selected to use for pendant being sure to mix in any add-ins into any of your colors. We used clear resin with chunky gold glitter for center color on our piece.

Step 3: Pour first color resin into spire mold filling ⅕ of the way up.

Step 4: Cure your piece under the UV lamp for 1 minute. You do not want the resin to be fully cured because it will begin to pull away from the mold. You just want the surface to be a little firm so colors don't mix.

Step 5: Pour next color resin into mold filling the next ⅕ of the way up.

Step 6: Cure your piece under the UV lamp for 1 minute.

Steps 7–10: Repeat Steps 5 and 6 twice.

Step 11: Pour your final color resin into mold filling to the top.

Step 12: Set your piece under the UV light for 2 to 4 minutes or as directed on your resin instructions. Flip the mold to make sure the bottom has a solid cure. Before you remove your piece from the mold, touch an inconspicuous place with a toothpick to be sure it has completely cured. If piece is still tacky, place in sunlight until hardened. Once completely hardened remove from mold. Deeper molds may take a bit longer to cure. For this shape of mold, roll sides down a little bit and pull piece out or use soapy water to remove.

Step 13: To attach the jump ring to top of pendant, cover entire top of pendant with clear resin. Holding jump ring in place with jewelry pliers, cure under UV lamp. Sand any sharp edges if needed with fine grit sand paper. Slide necklace chain through attached jump ring.

7

Spoon in Resin
TECHNIQUE

While this particular technique may sound like it would result in messy looking pieces, we have created some wonderfully detailed and rich color combinations to highlight the refined looks that can be achieved. This technique can be used in any shape and a variety of applications.

SUPPLIES

- Clear UV Resin
- Colorant or Pre-colored Resin
- UV Lamp
- Silicone Molds
- Plastic Gloves
- Silicone Mixing Cups
- Silicone Mat
- Plastic Spoons
- Tweezers
- Toothpick
- Fine Grit Sandpaper
- Necklace Chain
- Jump Rings
- Flat Sided Earring Studs
- Jewelry Snips
- Jewelry Pliers

Hoop Earrings

Step 1: Decide which mold shape you are going to use. We used an open sided hexagon shaped mold. Gather your supplies and lay out your silicone mat. Be sure you wear gloves to protect your hands while working.

Step 2: In different silicone mixing cups, mix all colors you want to use at one time.

Step 3: Spoon in small amounts of resin into the mold. If colors are mixing too much, you can cure for one minute after each color. Add in paper or glitter as desired.

Step 4: Quickly skim the top of the resin with a flame from a lighter to remove any bubbles from the surface.

Step 5: Set your piece under the UV light for 2 to 4 minutes or as directed on your resin instructions. Flip the mold to make sure the bottom has a solid cure. Before you remove your piece from the mold, touch an inconspicuous place with a toothpick to be sure it has completely cured. If piece is still tacky, place in sunlight until hardened. Once completely hardened remove from mold.

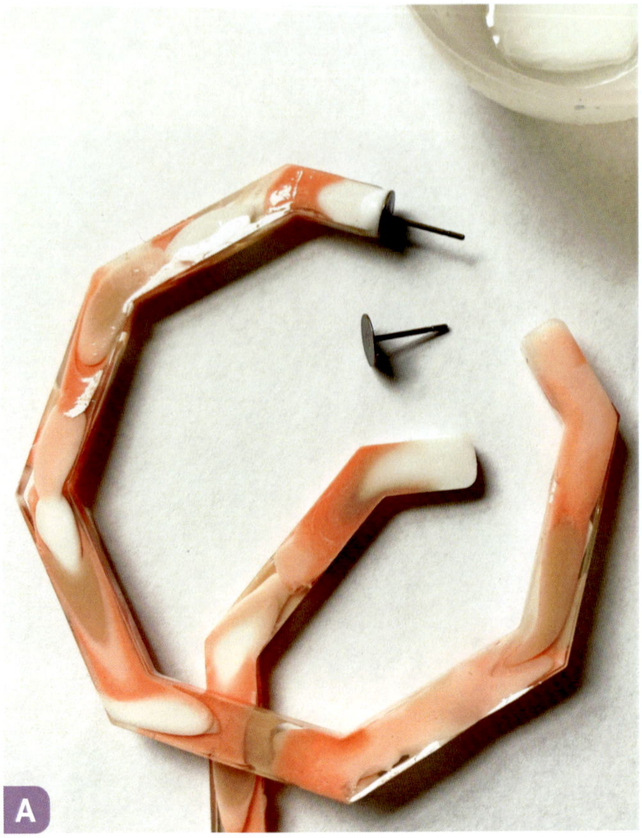

A

Step 6: If your piece has a slight dip on top, fill this area with a small layer of resin and allow to harden in sunlight. Sand any sharp edges if needed with fine grit sand paper.

Step 7: Using a drop of clear or matching colored resin as glue, attach flat sided earring stud to open end of hoop and cure under UV lamp again ***(photo A)***.

Swinging Earrings—2 Pair

Step 1: Decide which mold shapes you are going to use. We used long oval stemmed molds combined with small square stemmed molds for earring studs. For second pair we used odd-shaped circle stemmed molds combined with small circle stemmed mold for earring studs. Gather your supplies and lay out your silicone mat. Be sure you wear gloves to protect your hands while working.

Step 2: Mix the resin color you have selected to use for your earring stud circles.

Step 3: Pour resin into circle molds.

Step 4: Quickly skim the top of the resin with a flame from a lighter to remove any bubbles from the surface.

Step 5: Set your piece under the UV light for 2 to 4 minutes or as directed on your resin instructions. Flip the mold to make sure the bottom has a solid cure. Before you remove your piece from the mold, touch an inconspicuous place with a toothpick to be sure it has completely cured. If piece is still tacky, place in sunlight until hardened. Once completely hardened remove from mold.

Step 6: Set aside.

Step 7: In different silicone mixing cups, mix all colors you want to use at one time for swinging part of earring.

Step 8: Spoon in small amounts of resin into the mold. If colors are mixing too much, you can cure for one minute after each color. Add in paper or glitter as desired.

Step 9: Quickly skim the top of the resin with a flame from a lighter to remove any bubbles from the surface.

Step 10: Set your piece under the UV light for 2 to 4 minutes or as directed on your resin instructions. Flip the mold to make sure the bottom has a solid cure. Before you remove your piece from the mold, touch an inconspicuous place with a toothpick to be sure it has completely cured. If piece is still tacky, place in sunlight until hardened. Once completely hardened remove from mold.

Step 11: If your piece has a slight dip on top, fill this area with a small layer of resin and allow to harden in sunlight. Sand any sharp edges if needed with fine grit sand paper.

Step 12: Using a drop of clear resin as glue, attach small circles to earring studs and cure under UV lamp again.

Step 13: Using jewelry pliers, attach jump rings.

Colorful Pendant

Step 1: Decide which mold shape you are going to use. We used a rectangle stemmed mold. Gather your supplies and lay out your silicone mat. Be sure you wear gloves to protect your hands while working.

Step 2: In different silicone mixing cups, mix all colors you want to use at one time.

Step 3: Spoon in small amounts of resin into the mold. If colors are mixing too much, you can cure for one minute after each color. Add in paper or glitter as desired.

Step 4: Quickly skim the top of the resin with a flame from a lighter to remove any bubbles from the surface.

Step 5: Set your piece under the UV light for 2 to 4 minutes or as directed on your resin instructions. Flip the mold to make sure the bottom has a solid cure. Before you remove your piece from the mold, touch an inconspicuous place with a toothpick to be sure it has completely cured. If piece is still tacky, place in sunlight until hardened. Once completely hardened remove from mold.

Step 6: If your piece has a slight dip on top, fill this area with a small layer of resin and allow to harden in sunlight. Sand any sharp edges if needed with fine grit sand paper.

Step 7: Using jewelry pliers attach jump ring and slide pendant onto necklace chain.

8

Ombré Fade

TECHNIQUE

The ombré fade technique is a fabulous way to blend a variety of colors to any jewelry piece. We are showing earrings using clear resin with add-ins, as well as a blend of straightforward color to highlight this technique and the beautiful results. This technique can be applied in any shape or color you desire.

SUPPLIES

- Clear UV Resin
- Colorant or Pre-colored Resin
- Translucent White Resin
- Gold Glitter
- Iridescent Glitter
- UV Lamp
- Silicone Molds
- Plastic Gloves
- Silicone Mixing Cups
- Silicone Mat
- Plastic Spoons
- Toothpick
- Fine Grit Sandpaper
- Jump Rings
- Flat Sided Earring Studs
- Decorative Earring Studs *(with circle for attaching jump ring)*
- Jewelry Snips
- Jewelry Pliers

Pink to Gold Ombré Teardrop Earrings

Step 1: Decide which mold shape you are going to use. We used stemmed teardrop shaped molds. Gather your supplies and lay out your silicone mat. Be sure you wear gloves to protect your hands while working.

Step 2: In different silicone mixing cups, mix all colors you want to use at one time. We added chunky gold glitter into clear as one of our color choices.

Step 3: Slowly pour different colors into different sides of the mold allowing them to naturally blend.

Step 4: Quickly skim the top of the resin with a flame from a lighter to remove any bubbles from the surface.

Step 5: Set your piece under the UV light for 2 to 4 minutes or as directed on your resin instructions. Flip the mold to make sure the bottom has a solid cure. Before you remove your piece from the mold, touch an inconspicuous place with a toothpick to be sure it has completely cured. If piece is still tacky, place in sunlight until hardened. Once completely hardened remove from mold.

Step 6: If your piece has a slight dip on top, fill this area with a small layer of resin and allow to harden in sunlight. Sand any sharp edges if needed with fine grit sand paper.

Step 7: Using jewelry pliers, attach jump rings and secure attach pieces to earring studs.

Pink to White Ombré and White to Mica Ombré Earrings

Step 1: Decide which mold shape you are going to use. We used geometric shaped stemmed molds combined with small circle stemmed molds for earring studs. Gather your supplies and lay out your silicone mat. Be sure you wear gloves to protect your hands while working.

Step 2: Mix the resin color you have selected to use for your earring stud circles. For the White to Mica earrings we used translucent white resin with iridescent glitter chunks added.

Step 3: Pour resin into circle molds.

Step 4: Quickly skim the top of the resin with a flame from a lighter to remove any bubbles from the surface.

Step 5: Set your piece under the UV light for 2 to 4 minutes or as directed on your resin instructions. Flip the mold to make sure the bottom has a solid cure. Before you remove your piece from the mold, touch an inconspicuous place with a toothpick to be sure it has completely cured. If piece is still tacky, place in sunlight until hardened. Once completely hardened remove from mold.

Step 6: Set aside.

Step 7: In different silicone mixing cups, mix all colors you want to use at one time. For the top color on the White to Mica earrings we used translucent white resin with iridescent glitter chunks added.

Step 8: Slowly pour different colors into different sides of the mold allowing them to naturally blend.

Step 9: Quickly skim the top of the resin with a flame from a lighter to remove any bubbles from the surface.

Step 10: Set your piece under the UV light for 2 to 4 minutes or as directed on your resin instructions. Flip the mold to make sure the bottom has a solid cure. Before you remove your piece from the mold, touch an inconspicuous place with a toothpick to be sure it has completely cured. If piece is still tacky, place in sunlight until hardened. Once completely hardened remove from mold.

Step 11: If your piece has a slight dip on top, fill this area with a small layer of resin and allow to harden in sunlight. Sand any sharp edges if needed with fine grit sand paper.

Step 12: Using a drop of clear resin as glue, attach small circles to earring studs and cure under UV lamp again.

Step 13: Using jewelry pliers, attach jump rings.

9

Pictures, Drawings, and Dried Flower
TECHNIQUE

This technique is possibly the most personal and most rewarding section of all. Make any jewelry piece truly your own by adding pictures or drawings from your own family moments. We will also be explaining how to add dried flowers to your pieces.

SUPPLIES

- Clear UV Resin
- Colorant or Pre-colored Resin
- UV Lamp
- Silicone Mixing Cups
- Silicone Mat
- Stirring Sticks
- Toothpick
- Clear Packing Tape
- Fine Grit Sandpaper
- Small Paintbrush
- Acrylic Paint
- Tweezers
- Bezel Pendants

The Pictures/Drawings

Step 1: Decide which bezel shape you are going to use. We used closed back, square and round bezel pieces. Gather your supplies and lay out your silicone mat. Be sure you wear gloves to protect your hands while working.

Step 2: Cut out artwork you will be using just a little bit smaller than the opening of your bezel pendant.

Step 3: Press a piece of clear packing tape to front and back of artwork.

Step 4: Press down over the entire surface of taped piece to be sure no bubble were created when placing under tape.

Step 5: Cut shape out leaving just a small edge of tape on outside.

Step 6: Tuck your artwork inside of bezel piece. Trim if needed to be sure piece fits properly.

Step 7: Pour clear resin over artwork making sure it goes all the way to the edge and until full.

Set your piece under the UV light for 2 to 4 minutes or as directed on your resin instructions.

Step 8: Touch an inconspicuous place on bracelet with a toothpick to be sure it has completely cured. If piece is still tacky, place in sunlight until hardened.

Step 9: Arrange resin dots inside bracelet to be sure they fit properly before gluing into place.

Step 10: Using clear resin as glue, place a drop of resin to flat side of dots and arrange in place inside bracelet. Cure under UV lamp again.

Step 11: Pour clear resin over the entire inside of the dot filled bracelet cup to fill.

Step 12: Quickly skim the top of the resin with a flame from a lighter to remove any bubbles from the surface.

Step 13: Set your piece under the UV light for 2 to 4 minutes or as directed on your resin instructions. Touch an inconspicuous place on pendant with a toothpick to be sure it has completely cured. If piece is still tacky, place in sunlight until hardened.

Step 14: If your piece has a slight dip on top, fill this area with a small layer of resin and allow to harden in sunlight.

The Dried Flowers

Step 1: Decide which bezel shape you are going to use. We used a closed back round bezel pendant and a small sprig of baby's breath. Gather your supplies and lay out your silicone mat. Be sure you wear gloves to protect your hands while working.

Step 2: Paint the entire flower with acrylic paint. This can be done in any color you like. Set aside.

Step 3: Add a thin layer of colored resin to the inside of the bezel pendant being sure the resin goes all the way to the edge.

Step 4: Set your piece under the UV light for 2 to 4 minutes or as directed on your resin instructions.

Step 5: Touch an inconspicuous place on bracelet with a toothpick to be sure it has completely cured. If piece is still tacky, place in sunlight until hardened.

Step 6: Place flower inside bezel pendant.

Step 7: Pour clear resin over the entire inside to fill.

Step 8: Quickly skim the top of the resin with a flame from a lighter to remove any bubbles from the surface.

Step 9: Set your piece under the UV light for 2 to 4 minutes or as directed on your resin instructions. Touch an inconspicuous place on bracelet with a toothpick to be sure it has completely cured. If piece is still tacky, place in sunlight until hardened.

Step 10: If your piece has a slight dip on top, fill this area with a small layer of resin and allow to harden in sunlight.

Show us what you're working on!

Share your project photos with us on social media.
Tag us @leisureartsinc or use #leisurearts

Copyright © 2020 by Leisure Arts, Inc., 104 Champs Blvd., STE 100, Maumelle, AR 72113-6738, www.leisurearts.com. All rights reserved. This publication is protected under federal copyright laws. Reproduction or distribution of this publication or any other Leisure Arts publication, including publications which are out of print, is prohibited unless specifically authorized. This includes, but is not limited to, any form of reproduction or distribution on or through the Internet, including posting, scanning, or e-mail transmission.

We have made every effort to ensure that these instructions are accurate and complete. We cannot, however, be responsible for human error, typographical mistakes, or variations in individual work.

Made in U.S.A.